CAPTAIN MAKO'S
A to Z COLOURIN' BOOK O'
SEA BEASTIES

Copyright © 2024 Captain Mako

ISBN 979-8-9887310-2-3

Edited by Michael LoPresti and Maria LoPresti

Cover, layout, text, and artwork by Captain Mako

Published by

Rogues' Armada Press
PO Box 3037
Wakefield MA 01880
www.RoguesArmada.com

To order copies of this book or promotional items,
or to register for future updates, visit
www.SeaBeasties.com

Welcome Mates!

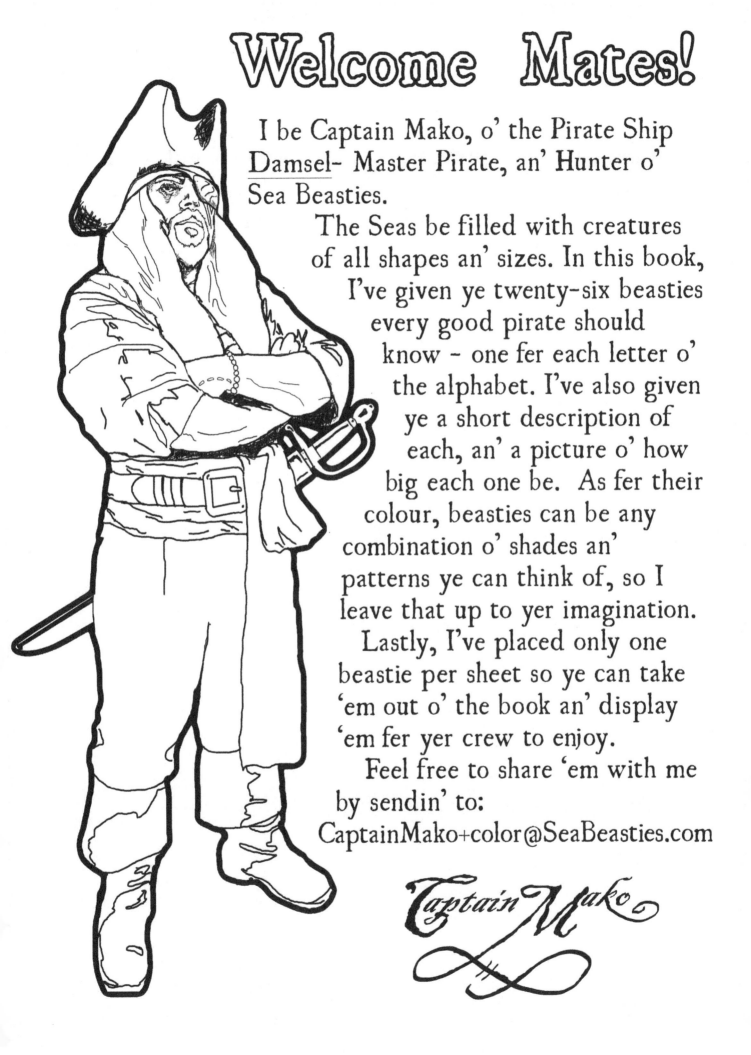

I be Captain Mako, o' the Pirate Ship Damsel- Master Pirate, an' Hunter o' Sea Beasties.

The Seas be filled with creatures of all shapes an' sizes. In this book, I've given ye twenty-six beasties every good pirate should know - one fer each letter o' the alphabet. I've also given ye a short description of each, an' a picture o' how big each one be. As fer their colour, beasties can be any combination o' shades an' patterns ye can think of, so I leave that up to yer imagination.

Lastly, I've placed only one beastie per sheet so ye can take 'em out o' the book an' display 'em fer yer crew to enjoy.

Feel free to share 'em with me by sendin' to:

CaptainMako+color@SeaBeasties.com

Captain Mako

Did Ye Know?

The youngest pirate on record were eight year old John King, who served aboard the Whydah Galley under Captain "Black Sam" Bellamy.

The ASPIDOCHELONE

Monstrous turtles what grow so large they be mistaken fer entire islands! They sleep fer centuries, durin' which time they become covered by trees, animals, an' even tribes o' people. You may land on an aspidochelone an' never know it – until the beast wakes up an' sinks into the Sea.

Pirate Joke

Q: What do marooned pirates eat on desert islands?

A: All the sand which is there.

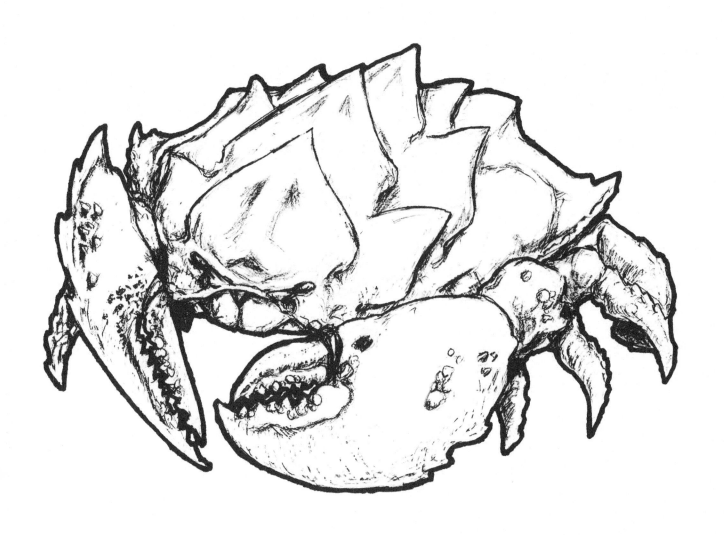

The BACHYURA

Bachyura measure eighteen to twenty foot across an' about fourteen foot high. They be eatin' machines, draggin' whate'er they can get their claws on into their maw an' grindin' it to sludge. But, though it be more monster than crab, the meat of a bachyura be a delicacy what will feed yer whole crew fer a week.

Did Ye Know?

A pirate flag , known as a "Jolly Roger", weren't always a skull an' crossbones on a black background. If a pirate flew a RED Jolly Roger, they meant business!

The CADDY

As sea beasties go, caddies be fairly common an' widespread. They ain't what ye'd call aggressive, an' they be more like to flee at the first sign of an approachin' ship, but they've strength enough to sink that ship, fer sure. Mostly night beasties, their large eyes be frightful sensitive to light.

165'

Pirate Joke

Q: What side of a parrot has the prettiest feathers?

A: The outside.

The DAGON

Dagons be an ancient race of intelligent sea cows. It be said that when the first humans learned to farm an' to sail, it were the dagons what taught 'em. Today, what few o' them remain tend to shy away from humans. But earn one's trust, an' ye may gain knowledge ye've never dreamed of.

Did Ye Know?

The most successful pirate ever may have been a woman from the South China Sea by the name o' Ching Shih. She commanded 1800 pirate ships an' 80,000 pirates!

The ENCANTADO

These beasties be a form o' boto – a rare, pink river dolphin o' the Amazon. But encantados have the power to shift into human form. Most often they appear as humanish dolphins, but once per year durin' Carnivale they've enough strength to become fully human, at least until the festivities end.

Pirate Joke

Q: Why did the pirate buy a new ship?

A: 'Cause it were on sail.

The FURNACE BIRD

One o' the strangest beasties in the Oceans, the furnace bird attacks with massive spines on its back an' powerful sickles where its arms should be. But most dangerous be the mane o' tubes on its head. From them tubes the furnace bird sprays super-heated sea water in all directions- hot enough to boil ye instantly.

Did Ye Know?

Pirates didn't only take gold an' silver. Sometimes it were more worth it to take food, silks, spices, black powder, cannon balls an' even medicine.

The GLOUCESTER SERPENT

This beastie made itself known to the fishin' town o' Gloucester Massachusetts many a year ago. Said to resemble a hundred-foot long string o' barrels with a parrot's beak an' wide eyes, the Serpent did little more than laze about the bay, eatin' a bit more than its share o' the local fish.

165

Pirate Joke

Q: What be the difference between a pirate
an' a cranberry farmer?

A: One buries their treasure.
The other treasures their berries.

The HIPPOCAMPUS

Not the half-horse with a fish's tail everyone thinks, hippocampuses be more like giant sea-dragons (which be a type o' sea horse). Used as ridin' steeds fer sea gods an' other powerful beings, these intelligent beasties be fiercely loyal to them what treat 'em proper.

Did Ye Know?

Most pirate ships were small an' agile. They needed to be fast enough to catch the giant Treasure Galleons an' nimble enough to make an escape.

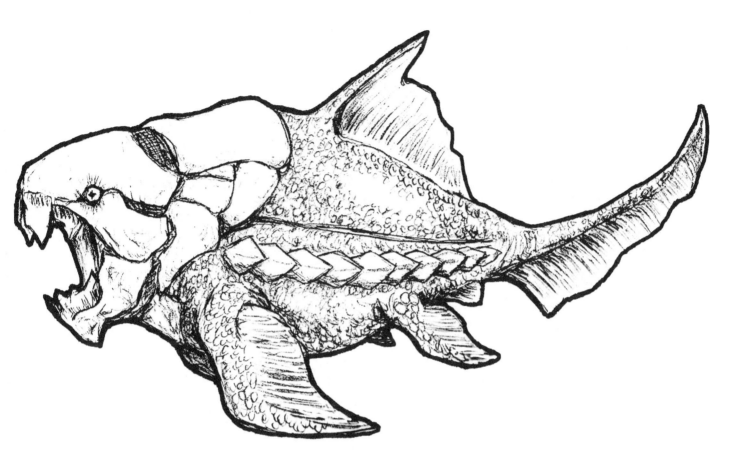

The IRONFISH

As their name suggests, the iron fish be covered in heavy plate scales as hard as iron, able to deflect even cannon shot. Their bite, pound fer pound, be one o' the strongest of any beast in the Sea an' allows 'em to easily chew through a ship's hull.

Pirate Joke

Q: Why couldn't the pirate play cards?

A: 'Cause he were standin' on the deck.

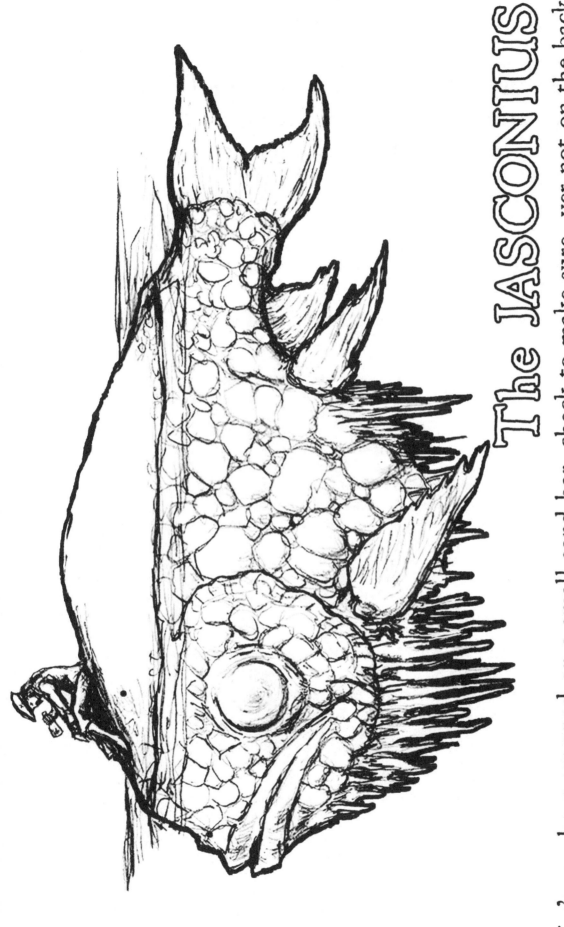

The JASCONIUS

If e'er ye be marooned on a small sand bar, check to make sure yer not on the back of a jasconius. They wait till yer weak, or sleepin', then dive below the waves to gobble ye up!

Did Ye Know?

A "Privateer" were someone given a special license by a government, called a "Letter o' Marque", to attack enemy ships. Basically pirates with permission.

The KRAKEN

Filled with rage, an' the desire to destroy any ship they come across, krakens have been the terrors o' the Seas fer thousands o' years. They can wipe away whole fleets with a sweep o' their giant tentacles. The only way to avoid an attack be to play possum. Krakens like their prey alive an' kickin'.

Pirate Joke

Q: Why does it take the pirates so long
to learn the alphabet?

A: 'Cause they spend years at C

The LOCH MONSTER

One o' the most famous but
elusive sea beasties, loch
monsters be tricky creatures.
They know yer out lookin' fer
'em, an' they enjoy playin' games
to keep from bein' found. They
can change their skin colour an'
texture to resemble mud, floatin'
logs, even sun-dappled water.
Ye'll only e'er catch sight o' one
if they want ye to.

165'

Did Ye Know?

Durin' battle, Blackbeard would tie hemp ropes into his beard an' hair an' set them on fire to appear like a demon to his enemies! DO NOT try that yerself!

The MERMAID

I suspect everyone knows what a mermaid be - lovely lasses with large fish tails. They enjoy sittin' by the shore, singin' songs to the crews o' passin' ships. But take heed. Mermaids, whilst kind-hearted, don't know their own strength - three times that of a human!

Pirate Joke

Q: Why don't pirates bathe afore they walk the plank?

A: 'Cause they'll just wash up on the shore later.

The NANUE (SHARK MEN)

When first born, nanaue pups look human (though ugly, if ye ask me). They can grow an' live their whole lives as humans, but should they eat meat any time after comin' of age, they'll become full-formed shark men.

Did Ye Know?

Hundreds o' words– includin' avocado, barbecue, breadfruit, cashew, catamaran, an' chopsticks – were introduced into the English Language by a pirate named William Dampier.

The OCULOPISCIS

Often called a "sea pig" because o' the gruntin' noises it makes, the oculopiscis be a huge monster fish. Its name means "eye fish" – an' true to it, the beast be covered in eyes what allow it to see in all directions at the same time. It will see ye long afore ye see it.

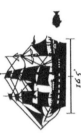

Pirate Joke

Q: How do ye make privateers?

A: Ye cry in a room by yerself.

The POLYPUS

Polypuses crawl about the ocean floor scavengin' whate'er falls to the bottom. But when a ship passes, they'll swim to the surface, latch on to the hull, an' climb on board. Their claws can crush through wood an' their shells can withstand all but the heaviest o' cannon fire.

Did Ye Know?

Every member of a pirate crew shared in the booty they captured. Crewmen received one share, skilled seamen an' officers got one an' a half, whilst the Quartermaster an' Captain received two shares each.

The QALUPALIK

People livin' in the Northern, frozen climes o' the world must stay on the lookout fer the qalupaliks. These beasts climb from the icy sea to capture humans, stuff 'em in the sack on their backs an' carry them off to their watery lairs. Keep yer encampments at least three hundred yards from water's edge.

Pirate Joke

Q: Where do ye find a pirate with no arms or legs?

A: Right where ye left him.

The RESPLENDENT ROSMARUS

The resplendent rosmarus measures nigh on forty-eight foot long. It gets its name from its armour, what resembles riveted bands o' silver an' turquoise, or sometimes purple an' gold. Ye may ne'er come across a beastie so full of itself. Within his own stretch o' Sea he may as well be an emperor – an' the emperor demands respect.

165'

Did Ye Know?

The idea o' pirates buryin' treasure probably came from
Captain Kidd, who stashed his treasure up an' down the
East Coast o' North America to avoid gettin' caught.
Most pirates just spent their treasure.

The SEA TROLL

Sea trolls make their lairs in underwater slime beds off the shores o' Scandinavia. As strong as an elephant, a sea troll can crack a ship's mast with its bare hands.

Pirate Joke

Q: What lies at the bottom o' the ocean an' twitches?

A: A nervous wreck.

The THALASSATYR

Thalassatyrs live in great underground villages where they keep vast stores o' treasure collected from ship wrecks. They be small beasts, but any pirate out to plunder should be cautious- they be strong enough to pick ye up with one hand an' toss ye up to ten foot away!

Did Ye Know?

Aboard a ship, cannons were called "guns" whilst handheld guns were called "pistols". The word "cannon" were only used when a gun were placed on land, or mounted on a building.

The UTELIF

Utelifs be the closest thing to a sea unicorn ye'll ever spy. The horn on their heads be edged with teeth like a saw blade so sharp it can slice through almost anything - includin' the belly o' yer ship!

Pirate Joke

Q: Why does a pirate carry a sword?

A: 'Cause the sword can't walk on its own.

The VEROSPHINX

This be the only species o' sea sphinx. Like their land cousins, they seek out an' guard places or items o' great value. When anyone approaches, the verosphix poses a riddle which must be answered. Answer correctly an' ye may be allowed to pass. Give the wrong answer an', well... ye don't want to know.

Did Ye Know?

The famous Captain Morgan was officially a privateer fer England, not a pirate, an' was even named Lieutenant Gov'nor o' Jamaica fer a time.

The WYVEREX

The only true sea dragons, wyverexes be livin' arsenals. They can swim as well as fly. A flap o' their wings will summon hurricane winds. Their fire breath will burn a ship to the waterline. Their scales gleam like gemstones. Mountains o' treasure be stored in their underwater lairs. But don't try takin' any, fer wyverxes can also read yer mind.

Pirate Joke

Q: Can pirates fire their weapons on Saturdays?

A: No, but they cannon Sundays!

The XYLOPOI

Xylopoi take the form of a human-shaped pile o' animated driftwood. Whether brought to life through magic or some other means I could not say, but they attack humans on sight. If ye can, burn 'em or chop 'em with an axe. Then maybe build yerself a nice table or some such.

Did Ye Know?

The word "pirate" comes from the 12th century Latin word "pirata", meanin' "sea robber". In Greek, the word comes from "peirates", meanin' "one who attacks." Fittin', don't ye think?

The YACUMAMA

Yacumamas protect the rivers where they dwell, an' everything what lives in them. Should one attack ye, they can suck up yer boat from a hundred yards away. If ye come across roilin' waters, there be a good chance a yacumama be near by. Blowin' a horn or conch shell will let the beast know yer only passin' through.

165'

Pirate Joke

Q: Did ye hear the joke about the pirate
who had no ears?

A: No, an' neither did he!

The ZITIRON

It be said that an encounter with a pod o' zitiron inspired
King Arthur to create his Knights o' the Round Table.
A sea knight be covered head to tail-tip in heavy, gleamin',
scaly plates. They live by a strict Code of Honour, an' they
don't care much fer pirates.

Did Ye Know?

The city o' Port Royal, Jamaica - a notorious pirate haven - was struck by an earthquake in 1692, which turned the sand to liquid an' sank it into the sea.

SPY THE DIFFERENCES

Take a gander at the two images below. The one to the left be meself, Captain Mako. The one to the right has ten differences about it. See if ye can spot 'em all.
(the answers be on the back)

1. Me eye scar be missin'
2. The bite mark on me hand be missin'
3. I've a double bracelet
4. The shine be gone from me sword pommel
5. Different shape to me belt buckle
6. The fold o' me sash be missin'
7. The sash be longer
8. No bell flaps on me boots
9. Me sword be shorter
10. Me beard be different

BEASTIE WORD SEARCH

Beasties can sometimes be hard to spot, so here be some practice fer ye. There be seventeen beasties from this book hidden in the puzzle below. I've given ye the list, but not the solution. Look hard, an' ye'll spot 'em.

```
D S O N N I R O N F I S H D R G Q E
E Q M B H O C U L O P I S C I S A O
N A N U E R U M H R K R A K E N L E
S H I P P O C A M P U S O V V Q U N
P C E M L O C H M O N S T E R M P C
O A F U R N A C E B I R D C P M A A
L D C F I H R P Q C D A G O N O L N
Y D T N G H M E R M A I D D N Q I T
P Y O C B V B A C H Y U R A G H K A
U H O A S P I D O C H E L O N E L D
S I O W D C J A S C O N I U S Z K O
G L O U C E S T E R S E R P E N T K
```

ASPIDOCHELONE
BACHYURA
CADDY
DAGON
ENCANTADO
FURNACEBIRD
GLOUCESTERSERPENT
HIPPOCAMPUS
IRONFISH

JASCONIUS
KRAKEN
LOCHMONSTER
MERMAID
NANUE
OCULOPISCIS
POLYPUS
QALUPALIK

Did Ye Know?

Comin' up with this many pirate facts be really hard.

STEER YER COURSE

As a pirate, ye must be able to sail yer ship through dangerous seas, avoidin' runnin' into beasties, 'til ye find yer treasure.

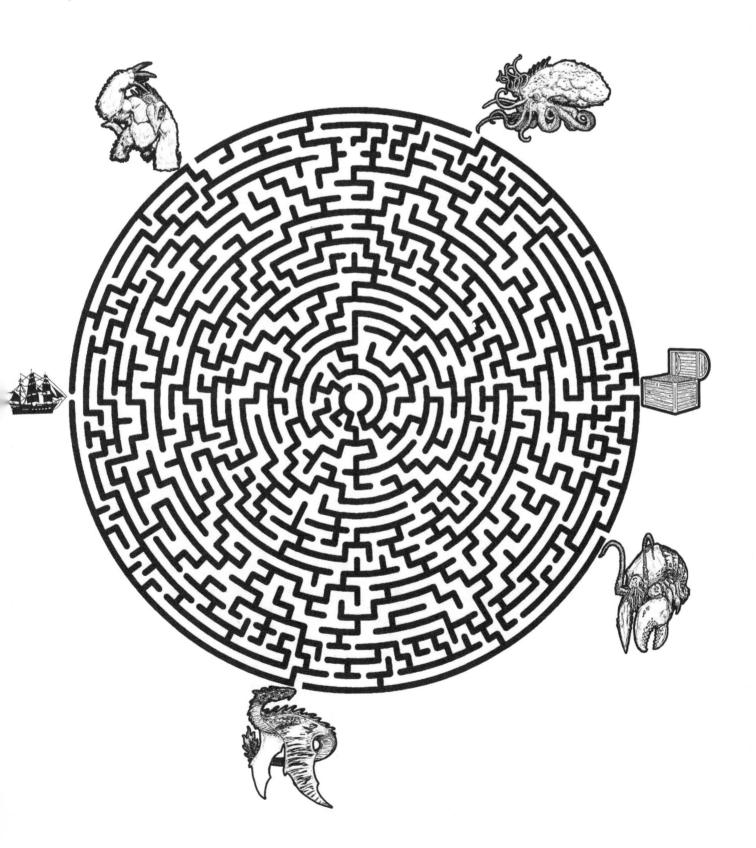

Pirate Joke

Q: Did ye hear the joke about the giant octopus?

A: Aye, it be kraken me up!

BUILD A BEASTIE

As I've said, sea beasties come in all shapes an' sizes. Draw yer own favourite beastie, or make up a new one!

Share yer creation with me by sendin' to:
CaptainMako+color@SeaBeasties.com

Made in the USA
Columbia, SC
05 July 2024

38163762R00037